changing the way the world learns

To get extra value from this book for no additional cost, go to:

http://www.thomson.com/wadsworth.html

thomson.com is the World Wide Web site for Wadsworth/ITP
and is your direct source to dozen of on-line resources.
thomson.com helps you find out about supplements,
experiment with demonstration software, search for a job,
and send e-mail to many of our authors. You can even
preview new publications and exciting new technologies.

thomson.com: *It's where you'll find us in the future.*

Critical Thinking:
Building the Basics

Donald E. P. Smith

University of Michigan

Glenn M. Knudsvig

University of Michigan

Timothy L. Walter

Oakland Community College

Wadsworth Publishing Company
I(T)P© An International Thomson Publishing Company

Belmont, CA • Albany, NY • Bonn • Boston • Cincinnati • Detroit
Johannesburg • London • Madrid • Melbourne • Mexico City • New York
Paris • Singapore • Tokyo • Toronto • Washington

Publisher: *Karen J. Allanson*

Assistant Editor: *Shannon McArdle*

Editorial Assistant: *Godwin Chu*

Marketing Manager: *Chaun Hightower*

Production Manager: *Stacey C. Sawyer, Sawyer & Williams, Incline Village, NV*

Interior Design: *Wendy Calmenson*

Print Buyer: *Barbara Britton*

Permissions Editor: *Veronica Oliva*

Cover Design: *Bill Stanton*

Compositor and Illustrator: *Rogondino & Associates*

Printer: *Edwards Brothers*

ISBN 0-534-19284X

Library of Congress Cataloging-in-Publication Data
Smith, Donald E. P.
    Critical thinking : building the basics
/ Donald E. P. Smith, Glenn M.
Knudsvig, Timothy L. Walter.
        p.   cm.
    ISBN 0-534-19284-X
    1. Critical thinking. 2. Critical think-
ing--Problems, exercises, etc.
I. Knudsvig, Glenn M.   II. Walter, Tim.
III. title.
BF441.S625   1997
160--dc21   97-42281
                                        CIP

For more information, contact
Wadsworth Publishing Company, 10
Davis Drive, Belmont, California
94002, or electronically at http://
www.Thomson.com/Wadsworth.html

International Thomson Publishing
    Europe
Berkshire House 168-173
High Holborn
London, WC1V 7AA, England

Thomas Nelson Australia
102 Dodds Street
South Melbourne 3205
Victoria, Australia

Nelson Canada
1120 Birchmount Road
Scarborough, Ontario
Canada M1K 5G4

International Thomson Editores
Campos Eliseos 385, Piso 7
Col. Polanco
11560 México D.F. México

International Thomson Publishing
GmbH
Königswinterer Strasse 418
53227 Bonn, Germany

International Thomson Publishing
Asia
221 Henderson Road
#05–10 Henderson Building
Singapore 0315

International Thomson Publishing
Japan
Hirakawacho Kyowa Building, eF
2–2–1 Hirakawacho
Chiyoda-ku, Tokyo 102, Japan

International Thomson Publishing
Southern Africa
Building 18, Constantia Park
240 Old Pretoria Road
Halfway House, 1685 South Africa

 This book is printed on acid-free recycled paper.

CONTENTS

PREFACE

Critical Thinking: Building the Basics is an easy-to-use, interesting book that will help you improve your basic critical thinking strategies. It is designed to be used across the curriculum in any course. Whether you are a student in a beginning English course or a freshman seminar, a graduate student in a psychology course, a medical school student, or an independent learner, you will find this book to be appropriate and user friendly.

How can any one book be appropriate to all students across the curriculum? We carefully assessed the basic critical thinking strategies that good students use and designed the book to teach these strategies. We tested the book on students at every level, from freshmen through graduate school. In doing so, we learned several important things from more than 2000 students and instructors who used the book. When we ask students what they could do better after using the book, they described several important outcomes. They now had strategies that helped them focus on information and organize it and process it in a new way that helped them think about and remember information better. In addition, the new strategies helped them make sense out of information that previously had been complex and difficult to understand.

By learning efficient and effective basic critical thinking strategies, students are in a position to learn higher level critical thinking strategies more easily. Without the basic critical thinking strategies, students struggle. That is why we designed the book. We saw students at all levels struggling unnecessarily. By spending a few hours working through *Critical Thinking: Building the Basics*, students gain basic critical thinking strategies that enhance their ability to focus, organize, categorize, process, and retrieve information. They think and learn information in more logical ways, which improves their ability to move up to higher levels of thinking.

This book is easy to use; it is lean and to the point. We have found that we can teach critical thinking strategies very rapidly. But to do so requires that students follow the instructions carefully and complete each exercise. As students complete the exercises, they can chaeck their learning by using the answer key to confirm that they are indeed learning the strategies.

Part I covers critical thinking strategies. Part II asks you to apply these strategies to your own work. We know that unless students can immediately apply these strategies to their own work, they are less likely to adopt the strategies as a lifelong means of thinking critically about everything they see and hear. It is for this reason that we have emphasized the across-the-curriculum approach to teaching basic critical thinking. When students see how easy it is to learn and apply the strategies to the courses in which they are enrolled, everyone benefits. This approach is far superior to teaching the strategies in isolation.

We want to acknowledge the more than 2000 students who worked through the various versions of this book to help us arrive at the leanest, most efficient and effective book possible. Many faculty and staff at public and private colleges and universities around the country have used the book with traditional and nontraditional learners. Whether at community colleges, small private institutions, or large state universities, the faculty and staff have been wonderful about using and endorsing the book. There are also several people we wish to thank whose reviews of the book have dramatically enhanced the creation of what they have called the "essential primer for critical thinking."

In particular, we would like to thank the following reviewers:

Anatole Anton, San Francisco State University

Robert L. Arend, Miramar College

Karen Beatty Sookram, Doane College

Kevin Galvin, East Los Angeles College

Randall E. Osborne, Indiana University East

Katherine Ploeger, CSU Stanislaus

Introduction

Some of you bought this book because the title and the description attracted your attention; it sounds like it will help you become a stronger thinker. Others of you bought this book because it was assigned for a course you are taking; in this case, the instructor wants to ensure that you have every opportunity to become a better learner and thinker. Whatever your reason for having the book, it is important for you to know that more than 2000 students from all around the United States have used earlier version over recent years and can tell you that it accomplishes what is intended: to help students learn basic critical thinking strategies, on which higher level thinking is based, and to make the thinking process more orderly and effective. Once you have learned the basic strategies, more advanced strategies will come much easier.

These students also helped us throughout the development process by providing valuable feedback on what was useful and what needed to be revised in each subsequent version. You are thus able to enjoy the benefits both of our own research as authors and teachers and of the experience of the many students who contributed ideas. This process of tryouts and feedback has enabled us to condense the book to a simple and understandable form. You can work through it on your own at your own pace, or you can work through it as part of a course.

The book is divided into two parts. Part I enables you to learn the basic strategies by applying them to material from a wide variety of subject areas. This part allows you to see how applicable the strategies are to every area of information you might need to deal with. Part II shows you how to apply the strategies to your own work and to the information you want to be able to think about, learn, and remember.

We have provided an answer key for many of the exercises. Learn to use this effectively so that you can get feedback on how well you are learning the strategies. The answer key will give you a sense of comfort, since you will know whether you are on track and making satisfactory progress. We—and many of the students who have used these materials—strongly suggest that you show friends, classmates, family members, and so on, what you are learning since this helps you check your own understanding. The more you share your learning with others, the more enjoyable and profitable it becomes for you.

PART I

A Basic Strategy for Learning and Thinking Smart

Do you consider yourself to be a really good thinker? a really good learner? And what about your instructors or your employers: do they consider you to be a good thinker? a good learner?

If you didn't answer with a loud *yes* to these questions, join the group. Most students often feel dissatisfied with the:

- **quality** of their work, of their output. They remember too many examples of

  —not showing that they can think clearly,

  —not giving good answers on essay tests,

  —not asking smart or useful questions in class,

  —not understanding something they have read,

  —not remembering what they heard in class.

- the **time** and **effort** it takes them to understand something, or to think clearly about a topic.

One of the problems is that much of what you are expected to do requires what are sometimes called *higher order* thinking skills (for example, analyzing, comparing, reflecting). But if you are like a lot of people you haven't had the opportunity to learn or to refine some of the basic "lower" and mid-level" thinking skills on which the higher levels build. "Many of you haven't yet developed any sure-fire strategies to help you acquire the basic information needed to operate at the higher levels.

A dominant characteristic of people who think smart and learn smart is that they seem to know what questions to ask at every stage when they are trying to learn something or to solve a problem. They know what information they need at each step as they work toward a goal—whether the goal is to relate lecture notes to a reading assignment, to contribute to a class discussion on a novel, to write a short paper, or to study for an exam.

In this book you will learn a strategy built around a series of questions that will help you:

- learn in a more efficient way,

- think more clearly and critically,

- proceed to more complex questions and topics,

- solve problems with more skill.

A Typical Student Situation

One of the most common situations facing you as you study, read, write, converse, or take exams is that you need to be able to understand, define, and describe the following:

- topics and subject matter that are fairly objective and straightforward (we didn't say *easy*, just *objective*)—for example, *the function of veins in blood circulation, steps in making a chemical compound, the parts of speech in a foreign language.*

- topics and subject matter that are less objective, less concrete, less obvious—for example, ideas and concepts such as *capitalism, global warming, welfare reform, genetic mutation, strategies for computer programming, fractal geometry, principles of physics.*

You may need to know these topics only "in isolation," that is, without having to relate them to other subject matter; or you may need to know them so well that you can relate them to other topics and deal with them on a higher level. Whatever the need, many students become discouraged because they can't seem to understand some topics clearly. They have not learned or been trained to think in a clear and focused way.

The strategy introduced in this book will help remedy this problem. It will help you obtain the critical information you need for starting to think about and work with a topic. It is built on asking, and trying to answer, several basic questions. This approach will work for you because (1) good questions help you identify the information you need and (2) the quality or completeness of your answer or information will give you feedback as to whether you are on the right track.

THE TCDR STRATEGY: TOPIC—CLASS—DESCRIPTION—RELEVANCE

To get you started right away, here is the strategy. Use it when you need to get a clear basic understanding of a topic, an understanding that will enable you to think about the topic in a critical and intelligent way. Always make sure that you ask and try to answer these **key questions** about what you are learning or investigating so that you will be able to relate or apply it to other material.

1. **What is the TOPIC I must understand?** (**T**CDR)

   What are the key topics

   —of the textbook chapter as a whole?

   —of the page I am reading now?

   —of the lecture as a whole?

   —of the lecture at this very minute?

   —of the broad issue we are discussing?

   —of the part I need to deal with right now?

2. **What is the overall CLASS to which this topic belongs?** (T**C**DR)

   —What is the whole of which this topic is a part?

   —What is the "main heading" under which this topic is being presented?

3. **What is the DESCRIPTION of the topic?** (TC**D**R)

   —What are its characteristics? its features? its properties?

   —What does it "look" like?

   —How would you describe it so that someone else would be able to recognize an example of this topic, whether in reading material, hearing about it, or on observing it in real life?

4. **What is the RELEVANCE of the topic?** (TCD**R**)

—What is its importance— to you, to other people, to some other topic being considered?

—What is it used for?

—What role does it play in understanding or explaining some thing else?

—How does it affect something else?

Look at this example of a simple piece of information that actually answers all four key questions.

A hammer is a tool, consisting of a handle with a heavy "head" placed on one end, used for pounding.

a hammer	the **topic** of the material
a tool	the **class,** the higher level, the main heading
a handle with a heavy head on one end	the **description,** the characteristics
used for pounding	the **relevance** or use

Practice Item Read the following definition and complete the matching task below:

A chair is a piece of furniture consisting of a horizontal surface supported by three or more legs and used for sitting on.

Match the items in column B to the correct label in column A by drawing a line between them.

A	B
topic	*used for sitting on*
class	*a chair*
description	*consisting of a flat surface, supported by three or more legs*
relevance	*a piece of furniture*

Reminder: Compare your answers with those in the Answer Key (p. 69) on practice items throughout the text.

As you proceed through this book you will receive lots of practice in using topic, class, description, and relevance. The exercises in Part I enable you to apply the TCDR strategy to information from texts chosen by the authors of this book; the exercises in Part II ask you to apply the TCDR strategy to information found in your own course texts or other reading assignments.

GOOD ANSWERS TO KEY QUESTIONS

As a student, the general question you will ask—and be asked—most often is the familiar *"what is x?"*, as in *"what is evaporation?"* or *"what is capitalism?"* Sometimes it is expressed as *"define x,"* as in *"define photosynthesis"* or *"define psychotherapy."*

Merely knowing the answers to these questions is seldom an end in itself (except on a test of definitions). Instead, the answers to such questions provide the basis for learning and thinking about related topics or for answering more complex questions. Nevertheless it is absolutely essential that you have good definitions. You need accurate information at this stage or any subsequent thinking or application will not only be difficult but quite likely incorrect.

You will be certain that you know at least the basics about any topic when you are able to give a definition of that topic that includes the answers to the four questions below.

1. **What is the topic I must understand?**
2. **What is the overall class to which this topic belongs?**
3. **What is the description of the topic?**
4. **What is the relevance of the topic?**

Let TCDR work for you.

EXERCISE SET A: Introduction to TCDR

The first set of practice items is designed to allow you to become familiar with the four key questions introduced previously (pages 3 and 4).

Note: The following few items and some others throughout the book may be quite simple. This is intentional. Many students complain that practice exercises in their courses don't always help them learn because they can't understand the content on which the exercise is based. Thus we will always start with simple content and then move to more difficult content. In this way you can focus on the model being learned.

DIRECTIONS

The following three pages include a series of passages and a question based on each one. Three pairs of answers are given for each question. One item of each pair is a **good** answer and tells you what you needed to know; the other is **bad** and gives you incomplete information.

- Circle each answer as **good** or **bad**.
- Tell which of these pieces of information is missing from the bad answer: **topic, class, description, or relevance.**

Fish are animals that have backbones and are able to live in water throughout their entire lives. They breathe with gills rather than with lungs. In place of legs they have fins. Their bodies are covered with hard scales that overlap like roof shingles. They provide humans with one of their most important sources of food.

Question: <u>What are fish?</u>

good / bad   *good / bad*

1. a. Fish are animals that live in water and are used for food.

   b. Fish are animals that live in water and are a source of food. They have a backbone, gills, fins and a covering of scales.

What part is missing from the bad answer? _____

good / bad　　　　　　　　　　　*good / bad*

2. a. Fish are animals that live in water and have a backbone, gills, fins and a covering of scales. They're used for food.

   b. Fish are animals that live in water. They have a backbone, gills, fins and a covering of scales.

What part is missing? _____

good / bad　　　　　　　　　　　*good / bad*

3. a. Fish live in water. They have a backbone, gills, fins and a covering of scales. They're used for food.

   b. Fish are animals that live in water. They have a backbone, gills, fins and a covering of scales. They're used for food.

What part is missing? _____

Enraged by attacks on their revenue and their dignity, John's supporters marched on London in 1215 c.e. and were welcomed by the townspeople and clergy, who had also suffered from John's demands. The barons demanded that the king accept a charter that would limit his power. John roared angrily, "Why do they not ask for my kingdom?" but he had to yield. The document John signed was the Magna Carta, or Great Charter.

Question: <u>What was the Magna Carta?</u>

good / bad　　　　　　　　　　　*good / bad*

4. a. The Magna Carta was a document signed by King John that limited the king's power.

   b. The Magna Carta was a document that limited the king's power.

What part is missing? _____

good / bad　　　　　　　　　　　*good / bad*

5. a. The Magna Carta was a document signed by King John that limited the king's power.

   b. The Magna Carta was a docu- signed by King John.

What part is missing? _____

good / bad   *good / bad*

6. a. The Magna Carts was signed   b. The Magna Carta was a docu-
by King John and limited the   ment signed by King John
king's power.   that limited the king's power.

What part is missing? _____

Bromine is a heavy, dark orange liquid used mainly in making ethyl gasoline. Some bromine is used in making dyes and medicines called *bromides*. A large plant that takes bromine from sea water is located in Freeport, Texas. The world produces about 100 times as much bromine now as it did before the sea water process was designed.

Question: <u>What is bromine?</u>

good / bad   *good / bad*

7. a. Bromine is a liquid used in   b. Bromine is a liquid, heavy
making gasoline and   and dark orange, used in
medicines.   making gasoline and medicine.

What part is missing? _____

good / bad   *good / bad*

8. a. Bromine is a liquid that is   b. Bromine is a liquid, heavy
heavy and dark orange.   and dark orange, used in
making gasoline and medi-
cine.

What part is missing? _____

good / bad   *good / bad*

9. a. Bromine is a liquid, heavy   b. Bromine is heavy and dark
and dark orange, used in   orange. It's used in making
making gasoline and   gasoline and medicine.
medicine.

What part is missing? _____

DIRECTIONS

Read the passages and answer the questions for each one.

10. There are more than 30,000 different kinds of fish, many of which we use for food. A favorite sea food is salmon. Most salmon live in the sea, but they lay their eggs in freshwater streams. To reach fresh water, salmon swim upstream, battling rushing currents and leaping up swift waterfalls. During these upstream journeys, called runs, many salmon are caught in nets and traps to be canned for use as food.

What is the:
  1. topic? _____

  2. class? _____

  3. description as provided here? _____

     _____

  4. relevance as stated here? _____

     _____

11. Iodine is a chemical found in sea water and in stalks of kelp, a type of sea-weed. The kelp is dried and burned, and iodine is removed from the ashes. In addition, some kinds of seafood, especially shellfish like shrimp and lobster, supply iodine needed in the diet. The "iodine" that is used as an antiseptic is a solution of iodine in alcohol, better known as tinc-ture of iodine. Pure iodine is a silvery-gray flaky material.

Question: <u>What is iodine?</u>

One learner's answer: Iodine, which is contained in sea water, kelp, and shellfish, is silvery-gray and flaky. It is used as an antiseptic.

  1. Your evaluation of the answer: *good   bad*

  2. What part, if any, is missing?_____

  3. Now rewrite the answer to make it a good answer. (Note that there is no one best order for the information, except that the class should be with the topic.)

     _____

     _____

     _____

12. An Ordinary rain cloud is a form of moisture. It is made up of billions of tiny water droplets. Sometimes two tiny drops will bump together and make one larger drop. When the drops become so heavy that air drafts and winds cannot hold them up, gravity pulls the particles down to earth and rain falls. One result is that plants and animals can continue to live and grow.

Question: <u>What is rain?</u>

One learner's answer: Rain is a form of moisture essential to the life and growth of plants and animals.

1. Your evaluation: *good   bad*
2. What part, if any, is missing? _____
3. Now rewrite the answer to make it a good answer.

_____

_____

_____

EXERCISE SET B: Identifying Topic and Class

This series of practice items will focus on only **topic** and **class** so that their identification will become second nature to you. If you are to become a clear thinker, writer, and reader, you first must be clear about what the topic is that you are studying or discussing or incorporating into a larger problem or issue. Then you must carefully identify the class of the topic so that you can find the appropriate description as well as information on relevance.

An example: Two people discussing the topic of fishing might have some difficulties in communicating if they do not realize that one thinks of fishing under the category of a business and the other thinks about it only as a form of recreation. Clearly the information related to relevance would be different.

Another example: Both the description and the relevance regarding the topic of capitalism would include different information depending on whether it is being thought of as a political system or an economic system.

Note: The passages used in Exercise Sets B and C will be very short so that you can make faster decisions and get more practice. Later you will practice using extended passages from commonly used textbooks.

DIRECTIONS

One or more words are underlined in each of the following short passages. Based only on the content of the passage, determine if the underlined item answers the question "what is the topic?" or the question "what is the class?" Place a check by the correct choice.

1. <u>Trout</u> are game fish. Although most trout prefer fresh water, they are members of the salmon family.

    —— topic?

    —— class?

2. Trout are game fish. Although most trout prefer fresh water, they are members of the <u>salmon</u> family.

    —— topic?

    —— class?

3. Trout are game fish. One variety, <u>rainbow trout,</u> originally were found in western streams, but they have been stocked in eastern streams by fish conservationists.

    —— topic?

    —— class?

4. "<u>Steelheads</u>" are rainbow trout that are landlocked in lakes or that have gone to sea.

    —— topic?

    —— class?

5. "Steelheads" are <u>rainbow trout</u> that are landlocked or that have gone to sea.

—— topic?

—— class?

6. Although rainbow trout was the topic in number 3, it is the

_____ in number 5.

Therefore: **a word that is the topic in one instance can be the class in another.** This is one reason why you must be a careful thinker while studying or communicating with others.

7. Order these items from most general to most specific; 1 = most general, and 4 = most specific.

trout   ( )   salmon   ( )
steelhead ( )   rainbow trout ( )

Thus, each of the items can be either a topic or a class, depending on the context of what is being said.

8. Goats, like other <u>cattle,</u> have a stomach peculiar to grass eaters that allows them to share to store food for later chewing.

—— topic?

—— class?

9. Goats, like other cattle, are of several varieties. <u>Swiss goats</u> have pointed ears. <u>Nubian goats,</u> dark in color, have drooping ears, and are milk producers. The <u>third type,</u> which includes Angoras, is remarkable for its production of wool.

—— topic?

—— class?

10. <u>Goats,</u> like other cattle, are of several varieties. There are three subclasses of goats. Swiss goats have pointed ears. Nubian goats, dark in color, have drooping ears and are milk producers. The third subclass is remarkable for its production of wool.

    —— topic?

    —— class?

EXERCISE SET C: Categorizing Information

DIRECTIONS

In each of the following short excerpts from textbooks, one or more words are underlined. Decide which question the underlined word or words answer in the context of the passage. Place a check next to your choice. The first one is already done.

1. One of the instruments used to study the weather is the <u>barometer.</u>

    —— What is the relevance, or the use, of the topic?

    ——X What is the topic?

2. This chemical is <u>used in the manufacture of soap.</u>

    —— What is the relevance, the use?

    —— What is the class for the topic?

3. The location of any spot can be determined by using the fine lines <u>that crisscross the map from north to south and from east to west.</u> These lines are. . .

    —— What is the topic?

    —— What is the description?

4. The inhabitants of this region make a curious kind of music through the use of a wide variety of <u>instruments</u>. First, of course, is the drum which. . .

—— What is the description?

—— What is the class for the topic?

5. <u>Sandstone</u>, on the other hand, is formed from sediment cemented together as a result of pressure.

—— What is the description?

—— What is the topic?

6. The suit is constructed of materials designed <u>to protect people from the burning rays of the sun</u>.

—— What is the relevance?

—— What is the class?

7. With such extremes of temperature and lack of air pressure on the moon, people need such a suit <u>to stay alive</u>.

—— What is the topic?

—— What is its relevance?

8. Although most trout prefer fresh water, they are members of the <u>salmon family</u>.

—— What is the class?

—— What is its description?

9. A parking meter is a <u>device</u> that indicates the time spent by a vehicle in a parking space.

—— What is the topic?

—— What is the class?

10. <u>Cells</u> were first described by . . .

— topic?

— class?

11. A phagocyte is a <u>body cell</u> that attacks germs.

— relevance?

— class?

12. <u>It is resistant to both heat and chemicals</u>, so parts made from it are commonly found in production machines.

— description?

— relevance?

13. In addition to its other roles, petroleum coke is <u>used in the production of whetstone</u>.

— relevance?

— description?

14. Recovery of such chemicals from their natural states is <u>important for medical and scientific purposes</u>.

— description?

— relevance?

15. Such devices may be used to <u>filter out the blue light and thus bring out the white tone of the cloud</u>.

— relevance?

— topic?

16. The <u>pituitary</u> is one of the glands of the body. It produces a number of hormones which . . .

—— topic?

—— description?

17. Uranus is farther from the sun than is earth. If you have keen vision, you can sometimes see the planet <u>Uranus</u> on a clear night.

—— topic?

—— relevance?

18. The green coloring matter in plants is called *chlorophyll*. It is <u>found both in the leaves of plants and in the stem</u>.

—— relevance?

—— description?

19. The method by which a government controls economic activities is referred to as <u>regulation</u>.

—— class?

—— topic?

20. <u>Silicone</u> is the name applied to a large family of compounds.

—— description?

—— topic?

21. It is for this reason that such materials can be <u>used as containers to hold strong acids</u>.

—— description?

—— relevance?

22. The heaviest of precious metals is <u>platinum</u>. Only gold and silver are easier to shape.

    —— topic?

    —— class?

DIRECTIONS

The following items are designed to give you a chance to review the four categories of information from a different perspective. Choose one of each pair:

1. If you want to find the TOPIC, you could ask:

    —— What does it look like?

    —— What is it about?

2. If you want to find the CLASS, you could ask:

    —— What is it used for?

    —— What is a general name?

3. If you want to find the DESCRIPTION, you could ask:

    —— What does it look like?

    —— What is a good title?

4. If you want to find the RELEVANCE, you could ask:

    —— What is it about?

    —— What is it used for?

5. If TOPIC:

   —— What is it about?

   —— What is its purpose?

6. If DESCRIPTION:

   —— What are its characteristics?

   —— What is a general name?

7. If CLASS:

   —— Is it possibly a process or a method?

   —— What does it look like?

8. If RELEVANCE:

   —— What is this about?

   —— What is its purpose?

9. If DESCRIPTION:

   —— What happens first? What next?

   —— What is it used for?

10. If RELEVANCE:

    —— Why is it important?

    —— What does it look like?

DIRECTIONS

These passages name the topic and provide information for one other part of the complete definition. Decide which other part is included and put an x by that item.

1. Look for a piece of fine-grained, gray, or creamy-white rock. If it is rather solid but can be scratched easily with the point of your knife, this rock will probably be limestone.

    —— description?   ____ relevance?

2. There are several kinds of anemometers. The most common kind has three or four cups attached to short metal bars connected to a shaft. The wind, striking the cups, makes the shaft turn. . .

    —— description?   ____ relevance?

3. The anemometer is used to measure the speed of the wind.

    —— description?   ____ relevance?

4. Only about 3% of all salt produced is used on our tables. It is used in brines for refrigerating, in the manufacture of glass and soap, and in making many other chemicals.

    —— description?   ____ relevance?

5. Slate, the material of which some roofs and school blackboards are made, is a metamorphic rock.

    —— description?   ____ relevance?

EXERCISE SET D: TCDR in Textbooks

One of the most difficult of the four questions is often "what is the relevance or use of the topic?". It is easy to answer this question when you read or hear such things as:

X was developed in order to explain . . .

Y ensures that the data is reported correctly.

Z was designed to be used in preventing . . .

But often, especially when the topic is a concept, idea, subjective term, or the like, the relevance or use is not overtly stated. Instead it is implied by the context in which it occurs. In these instances, your role is to think about why the concept or idea has been introduced. What is its intended purpose or use in this context? How does it contribute to the discussion?

Needless to say, it does not do you much good as a learner and thinker to know only the description of a topic but not how it relates to or helps explain other topics. Thus you must try to determine the relevance. This in itself is a higher level thinking skill becuase it may sometimes require a good deal of analysis, synthesis, hypothesizing, inferencing, and relating.

In some of the practice exercises that follow you will have to read the passages carefully and think about what is the relevance or use of each topic.

DIRECTIONS

A. Read the textbook excerpt on pages 23 and 24 and answer the questions below based on what you read. Write your answers in the space provided. The passage is from a social science textbook.

This exercise also provides an example of the following point made earlier in the book: any item can be the topic at one point in the discussion and later be the name of the class for other items, which might also be considered "subtopics."

B. Indicate for each answer whether

  • you found the answer clearly stated in the text, or

  • you "had to think it up," or

  • you are not sure how to answer it.

IN TEXT   THINK IT UP   NOT SURE

1. What is the topic? *social science*

    What is the class?   ____   ____   ____

    What is the description? (Write answer below.)

                                             ____   ____   ____

    What is the relevance? (Write answer below.)

                                             ____   ____   ____

2. What is the topic?   <u>anthropology</u>   ____   ____   ____

    What is the class?   ____   ____   ____

    What is the description?   ____   ____   ____

    What is the relevance?   ____   ____   ____

3. What is the topic? *cultural anthropology*

                                             ____   ____   ____

    What is the class?   ____   ____   ____

    What is the description?   ____   ____   ____

	IN TEXT	THINK IT UP	NOT SURE
What is the relevance?	___	___	___

4. What is the topic? _sociology_   ___   ___   ___

What is the class?   ___   ___   ___

What is the description?   ___   ___   ___

What is the relevance?   ___   ___   ___

5. What is the topic? _stratification_   ___   ___   ___

What is the class?   ___   ___   ___

What is the description?   ___   ___   ___

What is the relevance?   ___   ___   ___

Power and the Social Sciences

Social science is the study of human behavior. Actually, there are several social sciences, each specializing in a particular aspect of human behavior and each using different concepts, methods, and data in its studies. Anthropology, sociology, economics, psychology, political science, and history have developed into separate "disciplines," but all share an interest in human behavior.

Power is *not* the central concern of the social sciences, yet all the social sciences deal with power in one form or another. Each of the social sciences contributes to an understanding of the forces that modify the conduct of individuals, control their behavior, and shape their lives. Thus, to fully understand power in society, we must approach this topic in an *interdisciplinary* fashion—using ideas, methods, data, and findings from all the social sciences.

Anthropology

Anthropology is the study of people and their ways of life. It is the most comprehensive of the social sciences. Some anthropologists are concerned primarily with people's biological and physical characteristics: this field is called *physical anthropology.* Other anthropologists are interested primarily in the ways of life of both ancient and modern peoples; this field is called *cultural anthropology.*

Culture is all the common patterns and ways of living that characterize society. The anthropologist tries to describe and explain a great many things: child rearing and education; family arrangements; language and communication; technology; ways of making a living; the distribution of work; religious beliefs and values; social life; leadership patterns; and power structures.

Power is part of the culture or the way of life of a people. Power is exercised in all societies, because all societies have systems of rewards and sanctions designed to control the behavior of their members. Perhaps the most enduring structure of power in society is the family: power is exercised within the family when patterns of dominance and submission are established between male and female and parents and children. Societies also develop structures of power outside the family to maintain peace and order among their members; to organize individuals to accomplish large-scale tasks; to defend themselves against attack; and even to wage war and exploit other peoples.

In our study of power and culture, we shall examine how cultural patterns determine power relationships. We shall examine patterns of authority in traditional and modern families and the changing power rule of women in society. We shall examine the origins and development of power relationships, illustrating them with examples of societies in which power is organized by family and kinship group (polar Eskimos), by tribe (Crow Indians), and by the state (the Aztec empire). Finally, as a case study, we shall look at the controversy over "sociobiology"—that is, the extent to which genetics or culture determines behaviors.

Sociology

Sociology is the study of relationships among individuals and groups. Sociologists describe the structure of formal and informal groups, their functions and purposes, and how they change over time. They study social institutions (such as families, schools, churches), social processes (for example, conflict, competition, assimilation, change), and social problems (crime, race relations, poverty, and so forth). Sociologists also study social classes.

All societies have some system of classifying and ranking their members—a system of *stratification*. In modern industrial societies, social status is associated with the various roles that individuals play in the economic system. Individuals are ranked according to how they make their living and the control they exercise over the living of others. Stratification into social classes is determined largely on the basis of occupation and control of economic resources.

Power derives from social status, prestige, and respect, as well as from control of economic resources. Thus, the stratification system involves the unequal distribution of power.

DIRECTIONS

The next three passages are from a chapter in an astronomy textbook.

A. Define the topics <u>comet</u> and <u>comet nucleus</u> by answering the questions listed below. Write your answers in the space provided.

B. Indicate for each answer whether:

- you found the answer clearly stated in the text, or
- you "had to think it up," or
- you are not sure how to answer it.

	IN TEXT	THINK IT UP	NOT SURE
1. What is the topic? *comet*	____	____	____
What is the class?	____	____	____
What is the description?	____	____	____

IN TEXT   THINK IT UP   NOT SURE

What is the relevance?   ____   ____   ____

2. What other topics that are equivalent to comets would you
    expect to find in this chapter? _____

    _____

3. What is the topic? *comet nucleus*   ____   ____   ____

    What is the class?   ____   ____   ____

    What is the description?   ____   ____   ____

    What is the relevance?   ____   ____   ____

Comets

Comets are the most spectacular of the small bodies in the solar system.
When they pass through the inner solar system near the Earth, they can be
seen drifting slowly from night to night among the stars. (Writers sometimes
incorrectly describe comets as "flashing cross the sky" like shooting stars.
They do not. They seem to hang motionless and ghostly among the stars.
Their motion relative to the stars can be detected by the naked eye only after
a few hours.)

Comets have several parts, as seen in Figure 13-2 and 13-3. The bright-
est part is the comet head. The comet tail is a fainter glow extending out of
the head, usually pointing away from the Sun. Although a typical comet tail
can be traced for only a few degrees by the naked eye, binoculars or long-
exposure photos may reveal fainter extensions of the tail extending tens of
degrees or even extending clear across the night sky. A telescope reveals a
brilliant, starlike point at the center of the comet head. At the center of this
bright point is the comet nucleus, which is the only substantial, solid part of
the comet, but is tool small to be resolved by telescopes on Earth. Studies

reveal that a typical comet nucleus is a worldlet of dirty ice only about 1 to 20 km (a few miles) across—tiny compared to most planets and moons! The gas and dust that make up the rest of the comet's head and tail are material emitted from the nucleus. As the comet nucleus moves through the inner solar system, the sunlight warms it and causes the ice to evaporate into the form of gas. This gas, together with dislodged dust grains from the dirt in the nucleus, is then carried away. . .

DIRECTIONS

A. Define <u>photometry</u> by answering the questions after the following excerpt. This, too, is from the astronomy textbook.

B. In the space that follows the excerpt, write three other questions that the passage answers.

Photometry

Pictures of astronomical objects are interesting, of course, but much astronomical work requires measuring an object's brightness—the amount of light coming from it at all wavelengths or at selected ranges of wavelengths (such as blue to green). This is called photometry. By giving a precise measure of the amount of light at various wavelengths, photometry allows astronomers to measure temperature, composition, and other properties of a remote object. Until a few decades ago, this was done by measuring the size and density of the image on a photograph. Today it is done much more precisely with electronic devices. The basic device is a photomultiplier placed at the telescope's focus. Each photon of light collected by the telescope strikes the photomultiplier surface, which is designed to release a shower of electrons with each photon impact. In some designs, each electron strikes a surface and releases more electrons, thus multiplying the effect into a weak electric current that can be measured. Measurement of the current tells the number of photons arriving from the astronomical object, thus giving a measurement of its light intensity.

In recent years, these techniques have been extended into video-imaging devices that can produce TV images of objects too faint to photograph. Most important of. . .

	IN TEXT	THINK IT UP	NOT SURE

1. What is the topic? *photometry*   ____   ____   ____

What is the class?   ____   ____   ____

What is the description?   ____   ____   ____

What is the relevance?   ____   ____   ____

2. What are three additional questions answered by the passage?

DIRECTIONS

A. What is <u>planetology</u>? Define by answering the questions.
B. What is <u>comparative planetology</u>. Define by answering the questions.
C. Write one other question that the passage answers.

Comparative Planetology: An Approach to Studying Planets

Planetology is the study of individual planets and systems of planets. In the early years of planetary studies through telescopes, each planet tended to be characterized as a world unto itself: Certain markings could be glimpsed on Mars; Jupiter had a different type of markings; Saturn had rings; and so on. But in recent decades, as we have come to learn more about planets' surfaces, atmospheres, interiors, and evolution, with spacecraft and with sophisticated astronomical instruments, a new style of planetology has come into being. It is called *comparative planetology:* a systematic study of how planets compare with each other, why they are different, and why certain planets have certain similarities.

In comparative planetology, each planet and moon is regarded as an experiment that teaches us what type of environment evolves if you start with a certain mass, with a certain composition, at a certain distance from the Sun. A good example of this approach comes from . . .

_____

IN TEXT THINK IT UP NOT SURE

1. What is the topic? _planetology_   ____   ____   ____

    What is the class?   ____   ____   ____

    What is the description?   ____   ____   ____

    What is the relevance?   ____   ____   ____

2. What is the topic? _comparative planetology_ ____   ____   ____

    What is the class?   ____   ____   ____

    What is the description?   ____   ____   ____

    What is the relevance?   ____   ____   ____

3. What is one other question answered by the passage?

DIRECTIONS

A. Answer the two questions below with information from a chemistry textbook. (Write your answers in the space following the excerpt.) Remember that each of your answers is actually the answer to the four key subquestions. The two questions are:

"What is <u>filtration</u>?"

"What is <u>distillation</u>?"

B. Write an evaluation of each of your answers. Do each of your answers to "what is. . . . ?" answer the four key questions? If not, why not?

Separation of Mixtures

How would you (1) separate sand from water, (2) separate a mixture of water and ethyl alcohol dissolved in one another, (3) remove sand from table sugar, and (4) remove water from penicillin produced by a mold culture?

One of the chemist's most common problems is separating mixtures into fairly pure substances (Section 1.2) and then purifying these substances further. Some of the more common separation and purification techniques are (1) filtration, (2) distillation, (3) recrystallization, and (4) extraction.

Filtration

To separate sand from water, you could let the water evaporate, although this might take a long time and the water would be lost. You could also pour off the water (decantation), but unless done with great care some of the sand might be poured off with the water.

A physical process that avoids these difficulties is *filtration.* Like many methods for separating mixtures, it is based on the solubility of substances in a liquid solvent (Section 13.2). It can be used to separate (a) two solids if one is highly soluble in a liquid in which the other solid is insoluble or (b) an undissolved solid from a liquid. In this case, sand is insoluble in water and can thus be separated by filtration (see Figure 13.6). The mixture of sand and water is poured into a funnel fitted with a piece of filter paper. Sand, the insoluble component, stays on the filter paper, while the water passes through. The liquid that passes through the filter is called the *filtrate.*

Distillation

Sand can also be separated from water by boiling the water and then condensing and collecting the water vapor in a separate container. This process is called *distillation*. A simple distillation apparatus is shown in Figure 13.7. Such an apparatus is especially useful in separating mixtures of some miscible liquids that are soluble in each other in all proportions, such as water and ethyl alcohol, that have different boiling points. During the distillation process the ethyl alcohol, which has the lower boiling point, vaporizes more readily than the water. Thus, the liquid formed by condensing the vapor contains more ethyl alcohol than water. If this condensed distillate is redistilled, its vapor will be even richer in ethyl alcohol and the liquid remaining in the distillation flask will be richer in water. If this distillation and redistillation process is repeated often enough, the condensed liquid becomes almost pure ethyl alcohol and the higher boiling liquid left in the flask becomes almost pure water.

Your answer to "What is <u>filtration</u>?"

Answer to "What is <u>distillation</u>?"

Evaluation of answers: (Have you answered the four key questions in each of your answers? If not, why not?)

DIRECTIONS

A. Write an answer to each of the questions below on the basis of the information in the passage from an introductory psychology textbook. Write your answers and evaluations in the space following the excerpt. The questions are:

1. "What is psychoanalysis?" (or "Define psychoanalysis.")
2. "What is catharsis?" (or "Define catharsis.")
3. "What is free association?" (or "Define free association.")

B. Write an evaluation of each of your answers. Do they answer the four basic questions? If not, what proved to be difficult?

Psychoanalysis

Psychoanalysis, Sigmund Freud's method of psychotherapy, was the first of the "talk" therapies. Psychoanalysts try to help clients achieve insight into why they do what they do and think what they think (Figure 15.J) Psychoanalysis is therefore described as an "insight-oriented therapy" in contrast to therapies that focus on changing thoughts and behaviors.

Freud believed that psychological problems were the result of unconscious thought processes and that the only way to control self-defending behaviors was to make those processes conscious. Bringing them to consciousness, he thought, would release pent-up emotion in a process called *catharsis*.

At first, Freud sought to gain access to his clients' unconscious through hypnosis. He abandoned that approach, however, after he discovered that many clients immediately forgot the insights they had gained while under hypnosis. He developed other methods of bringing unconscious material to consciousness: free association, dream analysis, and transference.

Free Association

Free association is a method that Freud and his patients developed together. (Actually, a more accurate translation of the German expression would be "free intrusion.") In free association, the client lies on a couch, starts thinking about a particular symptom or problem, and then reports everything that comes to mind—a word, a phrase, a visual image. The client is instructed not to omit anything, not to censor anything that might be embarrassing, and not to worry about trying to express everything in complete sentences.

The therapist listens for links and themes that might tie the patient's fragmentary remarks together.

Your answer to "What is <u>psychoanalysis</u>?"

Your answer to "What is <u>catharsis</u>?"

Your answer to "What is <u>free association</u>?"

Evaluation of your answers: (Have you answered the four key questions in each of your answers? If not, why not?)

Question 1

Question 2

Question 3

DIRECTIONS

A. Read the following excerpt from a social science textbook and in the space following the excerpt write an answer to the question: "What is <u>fascism</u>?"

B. Write an evaluation of your answer. Does it answer the four basic questions? If not, why not?

Fascism: The Supremacy of Race and Nation

Fascism is an ideology that asserts the *supremacy of the nation or race over the interests of individuals or groups.* In the words of Benito Mussolini, "Everything for the state; nothing against the state; nothing outside of the state." The state is the embodiment of a unifying, ethical "ideal" that stands above the materialistic class interest of a marxist or the selfish individualism of the liberals.

Fascism perceives the state as not merely a governmental bureaucracy but *the organic life* of a whole people. According to Mussolini, "The Italian nation is an organism having ends, life, and means of action superior to those of the separate individuals or groups of individuals which compose it."

Answer to "What is <u>fascism</u>?"

Evaluation of your answer: (Have you answered the four key questions in each of your answers? If not, why not?)

DIRECTIONS

A. Underline in the following passage (from a psychology text-book) the information that seems to you to answer the question: "How are <u>primary groups</u> described?" (That is, find answers to "What is the description of <u>primary groups</u>?" or "What are the characteristics of <u>primary groups</u>?")

B. Then draw a wavy line under the information that seems to you to answer the question: "What is the relevance (impact/importance) of this topic?"

Primary and Secondary Groups

Not all groups are of equal importance to their members. For example, we will more willingly withdraw from a group made up of persons working in our office than from one made up of family or intimate friends. The notions of primary and secondary groups capture this distinction.

Primary groups are characterized by great intimacy among the members. People in these groups do not merely know one another and interact frequently but know one another well and have strong emotional ties. As a result, people gain much of their self-esteem and sense of identity from primary groups.

Moreover, sociologists regard the relationships among primary group members as the essential glue holding social life together. When Morselli (1882) and Durkheim (1897) blamed high suicide rates on modernization, they were claiming that, compared with traditional rural life, more modern societies have negative impacts on primary groups. These early sociologists also believed that people who lack primary group ties cannot obtain the social support needed to sustain them against trouble and despair. By now there is an immense amount of evidence that early sociologists were right about the dire consequences of social isolation. Indeed, sociologists have demonstrated recently that membership in a primary group even greatly reduces many "natural" causes of death (Litwak and Messeri, 1989). However, later in this chapter we shall see that Morselli, Durkheim, and other early sociologists were wrong to assume that modernization substantially increases social isolation: Even in the midst of large, seemingly impersonal cities, primary groups still thrive.

The family is the most common primary group, but many other groups can also become so. Indeed, Charles H. Cooley, who coined the term *primary group,* said a group is primary if its members refer to themselves as "we." Primary groups involve "the sort of sympathy and mutual identification for which 'we' is the national expression" (Cooley, 1909).

Secondary groups consist of less intimate social networks within which people pursue various collective goals but without a powerful sense of belonging. Business organizations, political parties, even model railroad clubs are typically secondary groups. People find it relatively easy to switch from one secondary group to another and refer to themselves and group members as "we" only casually. However, as we shall see in Chapter 20, primary groups often form *within* secondary groups—a process that can produce internal strains. For example, a group of close friends within a business may promote one another to the disadvantage of other employees and perhaps cause the company to operate less efficiently.

Groups, then, are the primary subject matter of sociology. The aim of sociologists is to construct a science of groups, of human social relations. However, not everyone believes that a science of social relations is possible.

DIRECTIONS

A. Underline in the following passage (from a psychology text-book) the information that seems to you to answer the question: "How is the similarity principle described?" (That is, find answers to "What is the description of this topic?") This is a topic in the section on Affiliation.

B. Then draw a wavy line under the information that seems to you to answer the question: "What is the relevance (impact/importance) of this topic?"

Affiliation

Affiliation is the motivation to be with others. Most of us like to be with other people, though not with just anyone. Suppose you are looking for someone to go to the movies with you or to be your lab partner in chemistry. How do you decide whom to ask? Four important influences on your decision are similarity, proximity, mere exposure, and physical attractiveness.

The Similarity Principle

If you could travel back in time and become close friends with any famous historical figure you chose, whom would you choose? Benjamin Franklin, Martin Luther King, Jr., Marie Curie, Agatha Christie, Confucius, Chief Sitting Bull, Susan B. Anthony, Joan of Arc, Sigmund Freud? Those are just suggestions; choose anyone you wish. How would you decide? Many historical figures would probably be interesting to meet, but in choosing a *friend,* you would probably look for someone similar to you or someone you would like to resemble.

How about your close friends? Do they resemble you in ethnic background, political and religious beliefs, academic interests, and attitudes toward sex and drugs? Most people choose friends who resemble themselves in many ways. This tendency is known as the similarity principle.

In one study, researchers at the University of Michigan surveyed 1,000 men living in or around Detroit. They asked the men to list their three closest friends and to provide information about themselves and about their friends, including age, occupation, religious affiliation, and political leanings. It turned out that the friends resembled the men on every variable that was measured in the study (Laumann, 1969).

Moreover, most people choose romantic partners who resemble them in various ways. Both dating couples and married couples tend to resemble each other in age, physical appearance, social class, ethnic identity, religion, intelligence, attitudes and values, and use or abstention from alcohol and tobacco (Burgess & Wallin, 1943; Buss, 1985; Osborne et al., 1978). Well-matched couples are more likely to stay together than couples who are not well matched (Hill, Rubin, & Peplau, 1976).

In a number of experiments to determine what role similar attitudes play in the attraction between people, pairs of subjects have filled out attitude questionnaires and then been shown what was said to be the other's responses. Actually, the experimenter falsified the responses in order to suggest a greater or lesser degree of similarity between the two. Then each subject has been asked how much he or she like the other person. The results have consistently shown that subjects like partners whose attitudes resemble their own (Byrne, 1971).

DIRECTIONS

A. Underline in the passage below (from a psychology textbook) the information that seems to you to answer the question: "How is group therapy described?" (That is, find answers to "What is the description of this topic?" or "What are the characteristics of this topic?")

B. Then draw a wavy line under the information that seems to you to answer the question: "What is the relevance (impact/importance) of this topic?"

Treating People in Groups

Freud and the other early pioneers of psychotherapy dealt with their clients on a one-on-one basis. Individual psychotherapy has its advantages, most of all privacy. But for many purposes it is helpful to treat clients in groups.

Group Therapy

Group Therapy is therapy that is administered to a group of people all at one time. It first came into vogue for economic reasons. Most psychotherapists charge substantial fees for the usual 50-minute session. (They have to charge more per patient than most medical practitioners simply because they see only one patient per hour.) Because middle-class and poor people in need of psychotherapy cannot afford those fees, some therapists began to treat small groups of people, spreading the cost among them.

Group therapy has other advantages as well. Therapists typically try to set up a group of about seven or eight people who are about the same age with similar problems—people who have as much in common with one another as possible. They take comfort when they discover that others share their problems. They learn from each other and are encouraged by each other's successes.

Group therapy sessions give people an opportunity to explore how they relate to others. Clients become aware of how they irritate others and how they can be useful to others. They use group therapy to develop and practice social skills (Bloch, 1986).

DIRECTIONS

A. This item focuses on description and relevance. Underline in the passage below (again from a psychology textbook) the information that seems to you to answer the question: "How is panic disorder described?" (That is, find answers to "What is the description of <u>panic disorder</u>?" or "What are the characteristics of <u>panic disorder</u>?") The beginning of the section on Anxiety Disorders is included to provide a context.

B. Then draw a wavy line under the information that seems to you to answer the question: "What is the relevance (impact/importance) of this topic?"

Anxiety Disorders

Many psychological disorders are marked by a combination of fear, anxiety, and attempts to avoid anxiety. Anxiety, unlike fear, is generally not associated with a specific situation. We feel fear in the presence of a hungry tiger, but our fear passes as soon as we get away. But we cannot escape the anxiety we experience about dying or about our personal inadequacies. Some degree of anxiety is normal; it becomes a problem only when it interferes with our ability to cope with everyday life.

Panic Disorder

Panic disorder is an emotional disturbance found in about 1% of all American adults and among very few children (Myers et al., 1984; Robins et al., 1984). People with this disorder experience a fairly constant state of moderate anxiety, along with occasional panic attacks, accompanied by chest pains, difficulty in breathing, increased heart rate, sweating, faintness, and shaking (see Figure 14.4). A panic attack generally lasts only a few minutes, although it may last an hour or more. During an attack, most people worry about fainting, dying, or going crazy (Argyle, 1988). After a few such attacks, those worries may grow more intense and may even trigger further attacks.

Panic disorder can become self-perpetuating (Figure 14.5). Many people deal with anxiety by taking a deep breath or two, to help calm themselves down. On the theory that "if a little is good, a whole lot will be better," they may continue breathing deeply, or hyperventilating. Hyperventilation expels carbon dioxide and therefore lowers the carbon dioxide level in the blood. Then if something happens that increases the carbon dioxide level, such as sudden physical activity or an experience that excites the sympathetic nervous system, the carbon dioxide level in the blood increases by a large percentage and stimulates an increased heart rate, trembling, and other symptoms of a panic attack—the very thing the person was trying to avoid (Gorman et a., 1986; Woods et al., 1986). After a few such episodes, the likelihood of further attacks increases. One treatment for panic attacks is to teach the person to avoid hyperventilating (Wolpe & Rowan, 1988).

When people discover that physical exertion sometimes triggers a panic attack, they may decide to avoid any sort of physical activity. As a result, they grow even more sensitive to the effects of physical activity; even slight exertion will raise the level of carbon dioxide in their blood. Consequently, some authorities recommend regular exercise as a treatment for panic attacks (Ledwidge, 1980).

DIRECTIONS

A. Underline in the following passage (from a social science textbook) the information that seems to you to answer the question: "How is <u>conservatism</u> described?" (That is, find answers to "What is the description of conservatism?" or "What are the characteristics of conservatism?")

B. Then draw a wavy line under the information that seems to you to answer the question: "What is the relevance (impact/importance) of this topic?"

Modern Conservatism: Individualism and Traditional Values

Conservatism and Liberalism

In the United States today *conservatism* is associated with classical liberalism. Conservatives in this country retain the early liberal commitment to individual freedom from governmental controls; maximum personal liberty; reliance on individual initiative and effort for self-development, rather than on governmental programs and projects; a free-enterprise economy with a minimum of governmental intervention; and rewards for initiative, skill, risk, and hard work, in contrast to government-imposed "leveling" of income. These views are consistent with the early classical liberalism of Locke, Jefferson, and the nation's Founding Fathers. The result, of course, is a confusion of ideological labels: conservatives today charge modern liberals with abandoning the principles of individualism, limited government, and free enterprise, and today's conservatives claim to be the true "liberals" in society.

Conservativism and Human Nature

Modern conservativism does indeed incorporate much of classical liberalism, but conservatism also has a distinct ideological tradition of its own. Conservatism is not as optimistic as liberalism about human nature. Traditionally, conservatives realized that human nature includes elements of irrationality, intolerance, extremism, ignorance, prejudice, hatred, and violence. Thus they were more likely to place their faith in *law* and *tradition* than in the popular emotions of mass movement. Without the protection of law and tradition, people and societies are vulnerable to terror and violence. The absence of law does not mean freedom, but rather, exposure to the tyranny of terrorism and violence.

Preference for Evolutionary Change

Conservatism sets forth an *evolutionary* view of social progress. Revolutionary change is far more likely to set back society than to improve it. But over time, people can experiment in small ways with incremental changes; continued from generation to generation, this process of evolutionary change leads to a progressive improvement in the condition of humanity. *No government* possesses the wisdom to resolve all problems, but the cumulative experience of society does produce certain workable arrangements for the amelioration of social ills. Gradual progress is possible, but only if people do not destroy the painfully acquired wisdom of the past in favor of new, untried utopian solutions that jeopardize the well-being of society.

DIRECTIONS

A. This exercise once again provides an opportunity to practice finding and writing answers to the four key questions. The passage is from a social science textbook.

"What is the topic?"

"What is the class?"

"What is the description of the topic?"

"What is the relevance of the topic?"

B. Evaluate the completeness of each answer. That is, to what degree were you able to answer each question?

C. Write three additional questions that the passage answers.

Automatic Stabilizers

Automatic stabilizers are government programs that act automatically to counter the effects of economic cycles. For example, since income taxes increase in proportion to one's earnings, the income tax automatically restricts spending habits in times of prosperity by taking larger bites of income. In times of adversity and low earnings, taxes drop automatically. Welfare programs also act automatically to counter economic cycles: in recessions, more people apply for welfare and unemployment payments, and those payments help to offset declines in income.

Monetary Policy

Since banks are the major source of money and credit, the government can control investment spending by making it easy to borrow money from banks. . . .

"What is the topic?"

"What is the class?"

"What is the description of the topic?"

What is the relevance of the topic?

Evaluate the completeness of each answer.

- topic

- class

- description

- relevance

Write three additional questions that the passage answers.

This is the final exercise for Part I.

DIRECTIONS

Here is one last practice item from a textbook on language learning. The topic of this passage is <u>conferencing</u>. The chapter title is "Writing as Process and Product"; this section deals with "Feedback on Written Work."

A. Circle the word or words that answer their question: "What is the class to which <u>conferencing</u> belongs in this particular passage?

B. Underline the information that seems to you to answer the question: "How is conferencing described?" (That is, find answers to "What is the description of <u>conferencing</u>?" or "What are the characteristics of <u>conferencing</u>?")

C. Then draw a wavy line under the information that seems to you to answer the question: "What is the relevance (impact/importance) of this topic?"

Feedback on Written Work

One of the most problematic areas in the domain of writing in a target language is that of feedback to the writer—whether it be from teacher, tutor, peer, or self. Let us first consider oral conferences and written comments from the teacher.

Conferencing

Conferencing, the term used to describe one-to-one consultation between teacher and student during the evolution of a composition, has become one of the buzzwords of writing (Graves 1983, Calkins 1986, Harris 1987). The concern for conferencing sessions is based on the position that an interactive session can help to clear up matters that cannot be handled by written feedback alone. There is, in fact, some research evidence that spoken feedback has advantages over written feedback (Rose 1982). Yet a major problem is that teachers need to find the time to conduct such interactive sessions. One large-scale study in Europe, for instance, found that most teachers do not have time for extensive individual conferences (Freedman 1987), but, even when they do take place, the reality of such teacher-student interactions may fall short of what experts would recommend.

PART II

Making the TCDR Strategy Work for You

As you learned in Part I, when you think about information in terms of **topic, class, description,** and **relevance (TCDR)** you will improve your efficiency and effectiveness as a learner and a thinker. Part II is designed to enable you to practice applying the critical thinking strategy of TCDR to material you will read in your own texts or hear in your classes. By doing so you'll see how appropriate the strategy is to thinking about any type of information you encounter in your courses.

You will find that by using this extensively tested strategy, you can produce the clear thoughts and the kinds of answers that will match those of the people you consider to be outstanding learners and students. The TCDR strategy will help you learn to think about topics in the ways your instructors and textbook writers do; you will be pleased to see how similar your questions and answers are to those of people you consider to be experts in the field.

EXERCISE SET A

Developing Questions and Evaluating Answers

DIRECTIONS

In Exercise Set A you can practice using the TCDR strategy on an excerpt of seven pages from *Introduction to Psychology* by James Kalat (pages 62–68). Read these seven pages and select several topics that you believe are important ones. These are topics that you might be asked to discuss in class or that you might be asked to relate to other topics for a paper or in an exam.

Your list of possible topics:

Good critical thinking requires that you determine which topics are most important or are most relevant to your purpose.

DIRECTIONS

Select from your list of topics one that you would like to focus on. (In this exercise you may select the topic primarily because of its interest to you, since you do not have a specific need at this moment.)

Your choice of topic:

As you saw in Part I, you can gain clearer understanding of important topics by using the TCDR strategy, first identifying the class to which your topic belongs and then gathering the information on description and relevance.

All the information you gather through TCDR helps you develop good answers to questions about the topics. These questions, many of which you may encounter in discussions, writing assignments, and tests, take many forms. Examples of these are:

- What is . . . (topic x) . . . ?

- Define . . . (topic x) . .

- Compare and contrast . . . (topic x and topic y) . . .

- Identify the important components of . . . (topic x) . . .

- What is the relationship between . . . (topic x and topic y) . . . ?

- Describe several examples of . . . (topic x) . . .

- What is the significance of . . . (topic x) . . . to . . . (topic y) . . . ?

Your ability to answer questions such as these about any topic you encounter can be increased greatly through the use of TCDR. Through this strategy you will obtain information that will demonstrate that you have thought critically and analytically about the topic(s) at hand.

If you review the questions at the end of textbook chapters, you will find that authors typically provide a variety of questions; some are very straightforward while others may be difficult to interpret. Whatever the form of the questions, TCDR will provide you with the basic structure from which to develop your answers.

DIRECTIONS

Write a question about the topic you selected (page xx). Base your question on one of the examples just listed.

Your question:

DIRECTIONS

Now, read the seven pages (62–68)to obtain the TCDR information about the topic before you actually write an answer to your question. You will first determine the **class** of your topic.

Write several possible classes to which your topic (your question) could belong and circle the class that seems most appropriate for this passage.

- _____

- _____

- _____

Now that you have selected a class, select from the material:

1. all the important **descriptors of the topic** and
2. all important information regarding the **relevance of the topic**.

Description

- _____

- _____

- _____

- _____

- _____

Relevance

- _____

- _____

- _____

- _____

- _____

Writing your answer

Now that you have determined the descriptors and relevance, it is time to write a practice answer in which you incorporate the necessary descriptors and any statements about the relevance of the topic.

Write your answer in the following space. Remember that you may not have been given all the descriptors of the topic in the pages you read. you may need to supply descriptors you are aware of from other sources of information. The same is true regarding the information about the relevance of the topic. The excerpt may not have addressed relevance as completely as you would have liked. Nevertheless, your answer may include information that you draw from other sources.

The important thing is that your answer should provide all the description of the topic that is needed and as careful a discussion of the relevance of the topic as is possible. If you have any question about this, check back to Part I to see how each answer includes as much discussion of description and relevance as is available and appropriate.

Your topic:

Your question (from page 3):

Your answer:

Your evaluation

Now it is time for you to evaluate your answer by responding to the following questions (referring back to Part I if you need to):

Does your answer describe the class to which the topic belongs?

_____ yes _____ no

Does your answer provide a good description of the topic?

_____ yes _____ no

Does your answer discuss the relevance of your topic?

_____ yes _____ no

What are other characteristics or special features of your answer that you think demonstrate good thinking and analysis?

• _____

• _____

• _____

Overall, what grade would you award your answer?

A _____   B _____   C _____   Other _____

Why?

_____

_____

Improving Your Thinking by Getting Feedback

Now that you have written your answer, we suggest that you seek another student's assistance to help you evaluate your use of TCDR. Ask another student with whom you feel comfortable in your course to work with you on this exercise.

Evaluation by a Classmate of Your Application of TCDR

Does your answer describe the class to which the topic belongs?

_____ yes _____ no

Comments:

Does your answer provide a good description of the topic?

_____ yes _____ no

Comments:

Does your answer discuss the relevance of your topic?

_____ yes _____ no

Comments:

Would you evaluate the answer as being worthy of an:

A _____   B _____   C _____   Other _____

Why?

_____

_____

More Points for You to Evaluate

1. If the excerpt provided the only information available to you, would there be enough information to answer the question as well as you would like, or would you need to seek information from other sources?

   _____ yes _____ no, I need to look at other sources.
   What additional information would you like to have?

2. Did you find that by using the TCDR strategy you were able to more rapidly structure your answer based on description and relevance?

   _____ yes _____ no
   Comments:

3. If you hadn't focused on description and relevance as you read the section, how might your answer have differed from the answer you wrote?

Thinking Point

Why do you think we first ask you to read a short section of a chapter and develop one good question and answer? If you start out by focusing on too much information at once you may be overwhelmed. Once you become comfortable with the TCDR process by focusing on small amounts of information you will be ready to tackle an entire chapter.

TCDR as a Cognitive Strategy

Learning to use TCDR is part of learning to develop what cognitive and developmental psychologists call a **cognitive schema.** A cognitive schema is just that: "a scheme," "a method," "a process" by which you can see, organize, and structure information so that you can understand and remember it better.

In Part II, as you continue using TCDR, the schema will become second nature to you. Whether you're reading articles from textbooks, journals, popular magazines like *Scientific American* or *Newsweek*, or any source, using TCDR will become the schema you use to think about things.

Note: One other point may interest you. Learners frequently complain that they have special difficulty analyzing and understanding certain textbooks and articles, or even lectures, even though they already know something about the subject matter. This may happen partly because the material is not well written or designed or is intended for a different audience. Everyone can relate to being assigned to read textbooks or articles that seem to have been written by professors for professors, rather than by professors for students. But making sense out of information that is poorly presented is another important strategy that you can acquire through TCDR.

TCDR: A Key to Strong Thinking

Your goal is to learn critical thinking strategies that will help you read, listen to, understand, and remember any type of information better. They key to your continued success will be to use TCDR whenever you read and listen. By always focusing on the basic questions posed by TCDR, you'll have a consistent strategy for interpreting, analyzing, organizing, and making sense of the hundreds of pieces of information that you encounter each day of your life.

As you work with and listen to strong critical thinkers, there is one characteristic that stands out: strong thinkers generally believe that an important part of the thinking process includes comparing their ideas with those of their peers. By comparing your answers and ideas with those of your peers and teachers, you will learn to attack problems and questions from different perspectives. You will see that many questions often have no one correct answer.

Strong critical thinkers are people who can take what information is before them and assimilate it into what they already know. They can accommodate information that is new or in conflict with what they know or believe. They develop answers, but are always ready to adjust their answers and perspectives based on new and valid information. This is why the great thinkers and scientists are people who may over a period of time shift their set of beliefs and sometimes take on radically different positions based on new information that contradicts their existing belief system.

Strong critical thinkers are the great creative problem solvers. They are people who are always open to new and different information. They are not tied to one position. They are willing to alter the way in which they see the world based on sound argument and information they collect from many different sources. They are open to assimilating and accommodating new information and to generating new ideas.

This process of thinking and rethinking is part of what education, experience, school and life are all about. You can learn a basic strategy, TCDR, for critical thinking that will dramatically improve your ability to think about information as you see and hear it. But, you must decide that, to be as strong a thinker as possible, you will always reexamine your thoughts and ideas; you will always be ready to listen to new and exciting perspectives and to adjust your positions or beliefs based on the best information available. Only then can you be a truly successful critical thinker.

Developing More Questions

At the beginning of Part II you developed a question and wrote what you believed to be a good answer to the question. Now pretend that you are the instructor of a course in psychology. Take the psychology textbook excerpt (pages 62–68) you read and say to yourself, "I am going to develop two more excellent short-answer questions from this section. These will be questions that I think a person reading this section should be able to answer."

DIRECTIONS

Develop two more questions and then use the TCDR strategy to complete answers to the questions. This is not meant to be a complex exercise. We just want you to see how easy it is to think clearly and effectively as you develop questions and answers that assist you in analyzing information.

Your two questions and their answers:

Learning from Another Person's Input

DIRECTIONS

Now that you have two more good questions and answers, share what you have done with a classmate who has gone through the same exercise. See what questions and answers he or she developed from the same material.

Evaluate each of your questions and answers:

1. Does each of your answers name the topic and class?

   _____ yes _____ no

2. Does each of your answers provide adequate description of the topic?

   _____ yes _____ no
   Comments:

3. Does each of your answers provide adequate discussion of relevance?

_____ yes _____ no

Comments:

Now that you have had a chance to use TCDR on a section of a textbook we have chosen, the next logical step is to have you choose a textbook from one of your courses and apply TCDR to information from a chapter that you are currently responsible for learning.

EXERCISE SET B

Another Strategy for Improving Thinking

DIRECTIONS

Choose a chapter from one of your textbooks on which you would like to practice using the TCDR strategy.

Write the name of your chapter you're using below:

DIRECTIONS

Check to see if there is a chapter summary at the end of the chapter. If so, please take a few minutes to read the summary. Research on thinking and learning has shown that people who read summaries can more clearly think about and more easily remember information on the important topics in a chapter. Summaries tend to focus on descriptions of important topics and discussions of each topic's relevance.

Did you find a chapter summary and read it?

_____ yes _____ no

Comments:

If yes, did the summary discuss the most important topics in the chapter, provide a brief description of the topics, and briefly discuss the relevance of the topics?

_____ yes _____ no
Comments:

DIRECTIONS

Check to see if there is a list of questions at the beginning or the end of the chapter; if there is, read these questions. These are questions the author thinks you should be able to answer if you understand and are able to think about topics within the chapter. These questions, just like the TCDR questions, will help you think critically about information and organize it into meaningful categories.

Did you find a list of questions and read them?

_____ yes _____ no
Comments:

DIRECTIONS

Now that you have read the summary and/or the questions and thus have a better understanding of what the chapter will be about, it is time to read the chapter. Go to the beginning of the chapter and choose a section of several pages that you will read.

What pages are you going to read? Pages _____ to _____.

Now read those pages.

From the pages you have read, select several important topics you would like to know more about.

Your list of possible topics:

Now select one of the topics you would like to focus on because of its importance to this section.

Your topic:

DIRECTIONS

Now write a question about the topic you selected that you think is important to answer.

Your question:

Now, from the pages you have chosen, gather the important information about the topic before you write an answer to the question. Please write this information in the space that follows:

CLASS

DIRECTIONS

Write in the possible classes to which the topic could belong and circle the class that seems most appropriate to the question you have asked:

1. _____

2. _____

3. _____

DIRECTIONS

Now that you have selected a class, select from the material (1) all the descriptors of the topic and (2) all important information regarding the relevance of the topic:

Description

1. _____

2. _____

3. _____

4. _____

5. _____

Relevance

1.   _____

2.   _____

3.   _____

4.   _____

5.   _____

DIRECTIONS

Now that you have determined the descriptors and relevance it is time to write a practice answer in which you incorporate the necessary descriptors and any statements about the relevance of the topic. Write your answers in the following space. Remember that you may not have been given all the descriptors of the topic in the pages you read. You may need to supply descriptors you are aware of from other sources of information.

The same is true of relevance of the topic. The pages may not have addressed relevance as fully as you would like, and you may decide to include information that you draw from other sources.

TOPIC

Your question (from page 57):

Your answer:

Evaluating Your Own Answers

Now it is time for you to evaluate your answer by answering the following questions:

Does your answer describe the class to which the topic belongs?

_____ yes _____ no

Comments:

Does your answer provide a good description of the topic?

_____ yes _____ no
Comments:

Does your answer discuss the relevance of your topic?

_____ yes _____ no
Comments:

What are other characteristics of your answer that you think demonstrate good thinking and analysis?

1. _____
2. _____
3. _____

Overall, what grade would you award your answer?

A ____   B ____   C ____   Other ____

Why?

Getting a Second Opinion

Now that you have written your answer, we suggest that you seek another student's assistance to help you evaluate your application of TCDR. Ask another student with whom you feel comfortable in your course.

Your classmate's evaluation of your application of TCDR

Does the answer describe the class to which the topic belongs?

_____ yes _____ no
Comments:

Does the answer provide a good description of the topic?

_____ yes _____ no
Comments:

Does the answer discuss the relevance of your topic?

_____ yes _____ no
Comments:

Would you evaluate the answer as being worthy of an:

A _____   B _____   C _____   Other _____
Why?

More Points for You to Evaluate

1. If the four pages you read were the only information available to you, would there be enough information in them to answer the question as well as you would like or would you need to seek information from other sources?

    _____ yes   _____ no, I need to look at other sources.
    What additional information would you like to have?

2. Did you find that by using the TCDR strategy you were able to more rapidly structure your answer based on description and relevance?

    _____ yes   _____ no
    Comments:

3. If you hadn't focused on description and relevance as you read the section, how might your answer have differed from the answer you wrote?

Developing More Questions and Answers

You have just developed a question and written what you believe to be a good answer. Pretend that you are the instructor of your course or the author of the book. Take the chapter from which you developed the question and answer and say to yourself, "I am going to develop five more excellent short-answer essay questions from this chapter."

DIRECTIONS

Using the TCDR strategy, develop five more excellent questions and then write answers to the questions. Write your questions and answers I the notebook you use for the course for which the textbook is assigned. As has been said, in developing your answers you may find that you have to go to other sources such as your course notes, other books, or your friends to find all the information you'll need to answer the questions correctly.

This is not meant to be a complex exercise. It is just meant to help you become comfortable thinking critically about an entire chapter. If you can use the TCDR strategy to analyze an entire chapter and develop five additional good questions and answers you will be well on your way to establishing excellent critical thinking skills.

Your Five Questions and Answers

-
-
-
-
-

An optional exercise

Now that you have five new questions and answers, it once again would be to your advantage to have a friend who is taking the same course review your questions and answers while you review his or her questions and answers. By sharing your critical analyses of what you think good questions and answers look like with your friends, you sharpen your critical thinking skills.

The dialogue between you and friends is part of being a critical thinker. Looking at one another's product, in this case questions and answers, will help you think critically not only about your own performance but about that of your peers. We learn to think critically by openly and honestly sharing our ideas and work. In this case, both of you have produced questions and answers. You now want to share your analysis of what you had to do to arrive at your answers.

As you discuss your questions and answers, you may wish to use the following questions:

1. Would I have answers as complete as the ones I just developed if I hadn't used the TCDR strategy?

2. What does having a "cognitive schema" of TCDR help me do as I read and listen to information?

3. What critical thinking skills would I *not* be using if I didn't approach reading and listening from a TCDR perspective?

4. Why is it easier for people to learn when they develop a TCDR "cognitive schema?"

5. How can I make myself comfortable with automatically using the TCDR strategy as I read and listen? Is there a specific procedure I can follow?

It's Time to Move On

You have done a lot of work in this book. It is no small task to work through all the exercises. But we have found that when students reach this point they are beginning to feel comfortable applying the TCDR critical thinking strategy to their daily course work. It is now time for you to move from this text to a daily routine of reading your course-related materials and listening to lectures and discussions using the TCDR strategy. You can always measure whether you are using the critical thinking strategy by asking several important questions:

- "What are the important topics of discussion?"

- "To what larger body of information or knowledge does this topic belong?"

- "How would I describe these topics?"

- "What is the relevance of these topics?"

- "What important questions can I answer about this infor mation?"

If these questions become part of your daily way of looking at and listening to your world, you will have mastered some of the basic steps of critical thinking. There is much more to the complex patterns of critical thinking than what we have described. But without being able to do what you have learned in these few pages, the more complex processes may well be difficult, if not impossible, to master. Congratulations on what you have accomplished so far. We hope TCDR makes your life, learning, and thinking more predictable, enjoyable, profitable, and exciting.

Reading Excerpt from *Introduction to Psychology* by James Kalat

How Thought Processes and Knowledge Grow: Some Piagetian Terminology

According to Piaget, a child's intellectual development is not merely an accumulation of experience or a maturational unfolding. Rather, the child constructs *new* mental processes as he or she interacts with the environment.

In Piaget's terminology, behavior is based on schemata. A **schema** is an organized way of interacting with objects in the world. For instance, infants have a grasping schema and a sucking schema. Older infants gradually add new schemata to their repertoire and adapt their old ones. This adaptation takes place through the processes of assimilation and accommodation.

In **assimilation** a person applies an old schema to new objects—for example, an infant may suck an unfamiliar object or use the grasp response in trying to manipulate it. In **accommodation** a person modifies an old schema to fit a new object—for example, an infant may suck a breast, a bottle, and a pacifier in different ways or may modify the grasp response to accommodate the size or shape of a new toy.

Infants shift back and forth from assimilation to accommodation. For example, an infant who tries to suck on a rubber ball (assimilating it to her sucking schema) may find that she cannot fit it into her mouth. First she may try to accommodate her sucking schema to fit the ball, if that fails, she may try to shake the ball. She is assimilating her grasping schema to the new object—expanding her motor repertoire to include it—but at the same time she is accommodating that schema—changing it—to fit the ball.

Adults do much the same thing. You are given a new mathematical problem to solve. You try several of the methods you have already learned until you hit on the one schema that works. In other words, you assimilate your old schema to the new problem. If, however, the new problem is quite different from any problem you have ever solved before, you modify (accommodate) your schema until you work out a solution. Through processes like these, said Piaget, intellectual growth occurs.

Piaget's Stages of Intellectual Development

Piaget contended that children progress through four major stages of intellectual development.

1. The sensorimotor stage (from birth to about 1 1/2 years)

2. The preoperational stage (from about 1 1/2 to 7 years)

3. The concrete operations stage (from about 7 to 11 years)

4. The formal operations stage (from about 11 years onward)

The ages given here are approximate. Many people do not reach the stage of formal operations until well beyond age 11, if they reach it all. Piaget recognized that some children develop at a faster rate than others, but he insisted that all children go through these four stages *in the same order.* Exactly how distinct the stages are is not clear (Keil, 1981).

The Sensorimotor Stage: Infancy
Piaget called the first stage of intellectual development the **sensorimotor stage** because at this early age (birth to 1 1/2 years) behavior consists mostly of simple motor responses to sensory stimuli—for example, the grasp reflex and the sucking reflex. Infants respond to what is present, rather than to what is remembered or imagined. Piaget concluded that infants in the senorimotor stage are incapable of representational thought—that is, they do not think about objects they cannot see, hear, feel, or otherwise sense. Moreover, Piaget concluded that infants lack the concept of **object permanence.** They do not understand that an object continues to exist when they can no longer see it. (Not only is it "out of sight, out of mind," but "out of sight, out of existence" as well.)

How, you might ask, can we possibly know what a baby does or does not think? We cannot—at least not for sure. Piaget was drawing inferences from the behavior he observed, though other people have drawn different inferences. After we review Piaget's observations, you can draw your own conclusions. (Better yet, study a baby to make your own observations.)

1. *Observation:* From age 3 months to age 6 to 9 months, an infant will reach out to grab a toy only if it is visible. If the toy is partially visible, the infant will reach for it. If it is fully hidden, however, the infant will not reach for it even after watching

someone hide it (Piaget, 1937/1954). *Piaget's interpretation:* An infant who does not see an object does not know it is there. *Other possible interpretations:* The infant may know the object still exists but may not remember *where* it is. Or the infant may be distracted by other objects that *are* visible.

2. *Observation:* If we hid a toy under a clear class, most infants will lift the glass to get the toy. If we hid it under an opaque glass, most infants will make no effort to get it. *Possible interpretation:* Infants do not ignore a covered toy because they are unable to remove the cover. They ignore it because they do not see it

3. *Observation:* If we show an infant a toy and then turn off the lights before the infant can grab it, the infant will still reach out to grab it in the dark (Bower & Wishart, 1972). *Possible interpretation:* Contrary to the first two observations, this one seems to indicate that infants will reach for something they remember but cannot see, provided they can see nothing else. In the first two cases, objects that remain visible may distract the infant from objects that are no longer visible.

4. *Observation:* From about 9 to 11 months, an infant who watches you hid a toy will reach out to retrieve it. But if you hide the toy first on the right side and then on the left side, the infant will reach out both arms to the right side. *One interpretation:* Even at this age, infants do not fully understand that an object remains where it was hidden. *Another interpretation:* Infants know the object has been hidden but cannot remember where.

The Preoperational Stage: Early Childhood

Around age 1 1/2 years, children reach a landmark in their intellectual development: They begin to acquire language at a rapid rate. Susan Carey (1978) has estimated that children between the ages of 1 1/2 and 6 learn an average of nine new words *per day*—almost one new word per hour—thereby increasing their ability to tell us what they know and think (see Table 1). The fact that they can now talk about the properties of unseen objects is evidence that they have acquired the concept of object permanence. But there remain many things they do not understand at this age. For example, they have difficulty understanding that a mother can be someone else's daughter. A boy with one brother will assert that his brother has no brother. A child may say that there are more girls in a class than there are children. Piaget refers to this period as the **preoperational stage.** The child is said to lack **operations,** which are reversible mental processes. For example, for a boy to understand that his brother has a brother, he must be able to reverse the concept "having a brother."

Table 1 Conversations with Some Children at the Proportional Stage

Q. Are you an American?

A. No, my father is an American, I'm a girl.

Q. Do you have to go to the bathroom?

A. Do Don't have to go. Mine peanut not working. Don't have any juice in it.

Q. Do you understand what's happening in this movie (a nature film)?

A. Yes. When the baby skunks grow up, they turn into raccoons.

Children at this age generally accept their experiences at face value. A child who sees you put a white ball behind a blue filter will say that the ball is blue. When you ask, "Yes, I know the ball looks blue, but what color is it *really?*" the child grows confused. So far as the child is concerned, any ball that *looks* blue *is* blue (Flavell, 1986).

According to Piaget, preoperational children lack the concept of conservation. Just as they fail to understand that something can still be white even if it looks blue, they fail to understand that objects conserve such properties as number, length, volume, area, and mass after the shape or arrangement of the objects has changed. They cannot perform the mental operations necessary to understand such transformations. (Table 2 shows some typical conservation tasks.)

For example, if we arrange two equal rows of pennies and ask which row contains more pennies, nearly all preoperational children will answer that the rows contain the same number of pennies. But if we spread one row out, they answer confidently that the longer row has more pennies. They do not even see a need to count the pennies to check their answer. Once we ask them to count the pennies, they discover that the number has remained the same (Gelman & Baillargeon, 1983). (Parents sometimes make use of a child's lack of conservation. A preoperational child has a cookie and asks for another one. The parent breaks the cookie in half and says, "Here. Now you have two cookies." At least some children seem satisfied.)

If we set up two glasses of the same size containing the same amount of water, and then pour the contents of one glass into a different-shaped glass, preoperational children will say that the taller, thinner glass contains more water.

I once doubted whether children really believed what they were saying in such a situation. Perhaps, I thought, the way the questions are phrased somehow tricks them into saying something they do not believe. Then something happened to convince me that preoperational children really believe their answers. One year, when I was discussing Piaget in my introductory psychology class, I invited my son Sam, then 5 1/2 years old, to take part in a class demonstration. I started with two glasses of water, which he agreed contained equal amounts of water. Then I poured the water from one glass into a wider glass, lowering the water level. When I asked Sam which glass contained more water, he confidently pointed to the tall thin one. After class he complained, "Daddy, why did you ask me such an easy question? Everyone could see that there was more water in that glass! You should have asked me something harder to show how smart I am!"

The following year I brought Sam to class again for the same demonstration. He was now 6 1/2 years old, about the age at which children make the transition from preoperational thinking to the next stage. I again poured the water from one of the tall glasses into a wide one and asked him which glass contained more water. He looked and paused. His face got red. Finally he whispered, "Daddy, I don't know!" After class he complained. "Why did you ask me such a hard question? I'm never coming back to any of your classes again!" The question that was embarrassingly easy a year ago had become embarrassingly difficult.

The next year, when he was 7 1/2, I tried again. This time he answered confidently. "Both glasses have the same amount of water, of course. Why? Is this some sort of trick question?"

The Concrete-Operations Stage: Later Childhood

At about age 7, children enter the stage of concrete operations and begin to understand the conservation of physical properties. The transition is not sharp, however. The ability to understand the conservation of various properties emerges sequentially at different ages. For instance, a 6-year-old child may understand that squashing a ball of clay will not change its weight but may not realize until years later that squashing the ball will not change the volume of water it displaces when it is dropped into a glass.

The **stage of concrete operations** is Piaget's term for the stage when children can perform mental operations on concrete objects. But they still have trouble with abstract or hypothetical ideas. For example, ask a child at this stage, "If you had five six-headed dogs, how many heads would there be?" Even a child who has no difficulty multiplying 5 times 6 is likely to object. "There there is no such thing as a six-headed dog!"

Or ask this question, "How could you move a 4-mile-high mound of whipped cream from one side of the city to the other?" Older children find the question amusing and try to think of an imaginative answer. But children in the concrete-operations stage (or younger) are likely to complain that the question is silly or stupid.

Or ask, "If you could have a third eye anywhere on your body, where would you put it?" Children in this stage generally respond immediately that they would put it right between the other two, on their forehead. They seem to regard the question as not very interesting. Older children come up with more imaginative possibilities, such as on the back of their head or at the top of a finger (so they could peek around corners).

Table 2 Typical Tasks Used to Measure Conservation

Conservation of number

Preoperational children say that the two rows have the same number of pennies.

Preoperational children say that the second row has more pennies.

Conservation of volume

250cc   250cc

Preoperational children say that the two same-size containers have the same amount of water.

Preoperational children say that the taller, thinner container has more water.

250cc   250cc

Conservation of mass

Preoperational children say that the two same-size balls of clay have the same amount of clay.

Preoperational children say that a squashed ball of clay contains a different amount of clay from the same-size round ball of clay.

Conservation of mass—water displacement

A child in the early part of the concrete-operations stage may know that a round ball of clay and one that has been squashed contain the same amount of clay.

However, the same child may think that the round and the squashed balls of clay will displace different amounts of water.

The Formal-Operations Stage: Adolescence and Adulthood The **stage of formal operations** is Piaget's term referring to the mental processes used in dealing with abstract, hypothetical situations. Those processes demand logical, deductive reasoning and systematic planning.

Piaget set the beginning of the formal-operations stage at about age 11. He attributed some fairly sophisticated abilities to children in this stage, although later research indicates that many children take much longer to reach it and some people never do get there.

Suppose we ask three children, ages 6, 10 and 14, to arrange a set of 12 sticks in order from longest to shortest. The 6-year-old (preoperational) child fails to order the sticks correctly. The 10-year old (concrete operations) eventually get them in the right order, but only after a great deal of trial and

Table 3 Summary of Piaget's Stages of Cognitive Development

Stage and approximate age	Achievements and activities	Limitations
Sensorimotor (birth to 1 1/2 years)	Reacts to sensory stimuli through reflexes and other responses	Little use of language: seems not to understand object permanence; does not distinguish appearance from reality
Preoperational (1 1/2 to 7 years)	Develops language; can represent objects mentally by words and other symbols; can respond to objects that are remembered but not present at the moment	Lacks operations (reversible mental processes); lacks concept of conservation; focuses on one property at a time (such as length or width), not on both at once; still has some trouble distinguishing appearance from reality
Concrete operations (7 to 11 years)	Understands conservation of mass, number, and volume; can reason logically with regard to concrete objects that can be seen or touched	Has trouble reasoning about abstract concepts and hypothetical situations
Formal operations (11 years onward)	Can reason logically about abstract and hypothetical concepts; develops strategies; plans actions in advance	None beyond the occasional irrationalities of all human thought

error. The 14-year-old (formal operations) holds the sticks upright with their bottom ends on the table and then removes the longest one, the second-longest one, and so on.

A second example: We set up five bottles of clear liquid and explain that it is possible, by mixing the liquids together in a certain combination, to produce a yellow liquid. The task is to find the right combination. Children in the concrete-operations stage plunge right in with an unsystematic trial-and-error search. They try combining bottles A and B; then C and D, then perhaps A, C, and E, and so on. By the time they work through five or six combinations they forgot which ones they have already tried. They may try one combination several times and others not at all; if and when they do stumble onto the correct combination, it is mostly a matter of luck.

Children in the formal-operations stage approach the problem more systematically. They may first try all the two-bottle combinations: AB, AC, AD, AE, BC, and so forth. If all those fail, they turn to three-bottle combinations: ABC, ABD, ABE, ACD, and so on. By adopting a strategy for trying every possible combination one time and one time only, they are bound to succeed.

Children do not reach the stage of formal operations any more suddenly than they reach the concrete-operations stage. Before they can reason logically about a particular problem, they must first have had a fair amount of experience in dealing with that problem. A 9-year-old who has spent a great deal of time playing chess, reasons logically about chess problems and plans several moves ahead. The same child reverts to concrete reasoning when faced with an unfamiliar problem.

Table 3 summarizes Piaget's four stages.

SOURCE: From *Introduction To Psychology,* Second Edition By James W. Kalat. Copyright © 1990, 1986 by Wadsworth, Inc., Pages 196–200 reprinted by permission of the publisher.

Critical Thinking: Building the Basics

Part I – Answer Key

Page Number	Exercise Number	Answers (and Comments)
		topic–chair; class–a piece of furniture; description–consisting of a flat surface supported by three or more legs; relevance–used for sitting on
6	1	1st answer bad; missing: full description of appearance
7	2	2nd answer bad; missing: relevance (doesn't tell what they are used for)
7	3	1st answer bad; missing: class (animal)
7	4	2nd answer bad; missing: description ("signed by King John" is the only description provided in the passage)
7	5	2nd answer bad; missing: relevance (the purpose was to limit the king's power)
8	6	1st answer bad; missing: class (It is classified here as a document and not, for example, as a law or command or decree.)
8	7	1st answer bad; missing: description ("heavy and dark orange")
8	8	1st answer bad; missing: relevance (does not tell what it is used for)

Page Number	**Exercise Number**	**Answers (and Comments)**
8	9	2nd answer bad; missing: class (does not tell whether it is a liquid or a solid or a chemical, and so on)
9	10	1. salmon 2. seafood, or fish 3. live in the sea; lay eggs in quiet freshwater streams, which they reach by swimming upstream from the sea 4. used as food for people
9	11	1. bad 2. class 3. for example: "Iodine is a chemical that is contained in sea water, kelp and shellfish. It has a silvery-gray and flaky appearance. It is used as an antiseptic."
10	12	1. bad 2. description 3. for example: "Rain is a form of moisture made up of billions of tiny droplets, which, when they get too heavy in the clouds, are pulled by gravity to the earth. Rain is essential for the life and growth of plants and animals."
11	1	topic
11	2	class
11	3	topic
11	4	topic

Page Number	Exercise Number	Answers (and Comments)
11	5	class
11	6	class
12	7	salmon 1, trout 2, rainbow trout 3, steelhead 4
12	8	class
12	9	topic
13	10	class
13	1	example (topic)
13	2	relevance
13	3	description
14	4	class
14	5	topic
14	6	relevance
14	7	relevance
14	8	class
14	9	class
15	10	topic
15	11	class
15	12	description
15	13	relevance
15	14	relevance
15	15	relevance
16	16	topic
16	17	topic
16	18	description
16	19	topic
16	20	topic
16	21	relevance
17	22	topic
17	1	What is it about?

Page Number	Exercise Number	Answers (and Comments)
17	2	What is a general name?
17	3	What does it look like?
17	4	What is it used for?
18	5	What is it about?
18	6	What are its characteristics?
18	7	Is it possibly a process or a method?
18	8	What is its purpose?
18	9	What happens first? What next?
18	10	Why is it important?
19	1	description
19	2	description
19	3	relevance
19	4	relevance
19	5	relevance

Note: We hope that you realized that the main topic is power and the social sciences. The practice items below examine some of the topics that support the main topic.

21	1	What is the topic?
		social science
		What is the class?
		Not stated in this excerpt—but social science is one of the three traditional divisions of academic study, together with the natural sciences and the humanities.

Page Number	Exercise Number	Answers (and Comments)

What is the description?

The study of human behavior; has several separate "disciplines" such as anthropology, sociology, economics, psychology, political science and history, and each use different concepts, methods, and data in their studies of behavior.

What is the relevance?

—to provide explanations of various aspects of human behavior

—"to contribute to an understanding of the forces that modify the conduct of individuals, control their behavior, and shape their lives."

21   2   What is the topic?
anthropology

What is the class?
social science

What is the description?

—In general, the study of people and their ways of life.

—Specifically, the study of (1) people's biological and physical characteristics and (2) the ways of life of both ancient and modern peoples.

Page Number	Exercise Number	Answers (and Comments)

What is the relevance?

—the overall topic of power will be examined from the perspective of each of the separate disciplines, in this case, anthropology.

21   3   **What is the topic?**

cultural anthropology

(Note: This is only a briefly mentioned topic, and should not distract the reader from the larger topic, anthropology, which is a subtopic under the broad topic of power.)

What is the class?

anthropology

What is the description?

the study of the ways of life of both ancient and modern peoples

What is the relevance?

—to better define anthropology

—to set the scene for the next topic, culture.

22   4   **What is the topic?**

sociology

What is the class?

a social science

What is the description?

the study of relationships among individuals and groups (All of the information in the paragraph describes what sociology studies.)

Page Number	**Exercise Number**	**Answers (and Comments)**

What is the relevance?
same as for anthropology, above

22   **5**

What is the topic?
stratification

What is the class?
a classification system

What is the description?
a system of classifying people according to their "ranking," which is determined by how people make their living, the control they have over the livings of others

What is the relevance?
a person's rank (in a stratification system) influences the amount of power he or she has (Remember: the main topic in this passage is power.)

24   **1**

What is the topic?
comet

What is the class?
bodies in the solar system

What is the description?
—comets are small bodies in the solar system; visible among the stars; seem motionless to naked eye (they do not flash like shooting stars)

—have several parts: comet head, comet tail, and comet nucleus (See topic next page.)

Page Number	Exercise Number	Answers (and Comments)
		<u>What is the relevance?</u> To answer this you would need access either to the end of this passage on comets or to the rest of the chapter.
25	2	What other topics that are equivalent to comets would you expect to find in this chapter? other bodies in the solar system
25	3	<u>What is the topic?</u> comet nucleus <u>What is the class?</u> comets, or comet parts, or composition of a comet <u>What is the description?</u> —located at the center of the bright starlight point at the center of the comet head —only solid art of the comet; a worldlet of dirty ice only about 1 to 20 km across, too small to be resolved by telescopes on earth <u>What is the relevance?</u> to provide a complete description of a comet head
27	1	<u>What is the topic?</u> photometry

Page Number	**Exercise Number**	**Answers (and Comments)**

What is the class?

a measurement system in the field of astronomy

What is the description?

measurement of the brightness of astronomical objects by electronic devices (*specific description is provided in passage—for example, "the basic device is a photo multiplier. . ."*)

What is the relevance?

allows astronomers to measure temperature, composition, and other properties of a remote astronomical object

27	2	

What are three additional questions answered by the passage?

Sample questions:

—How was measurement done previously?

—How does a photomultiplier work?

—Are there other uses for the technique?

28	1	

What is the topic?

planetology

What is the class?

This excerpt does not directly name the class other than to state that it is a field of study regarding planets.

Page Number	Exercise Number	Answers (and Comments)

What is the description?

the study of individual planets and systems of planets; the study, for example, of

surfaces, atmospheres, interiors, and evolution

What is the relevance?

Since this topic pertains to the "study of" planets, one of the purposes would be to gain more information about planets. The excerpt does not tell us what its role is in the larger context of the chapter.

28   2   What is the topic?

comparative planetology

What is the class?

a type of planetology; an *approach* to studying planets

What is the description?

a study of how planets compare with one another, why they are different, and why certain planets have certain similarities.

What is the relevance?

to be able to compare planets, rather than considering them in isolation as traditional planetology did

Page Number	Exercise Number	Answers (and Comments)

| 28 | 3 | <u>What is one other question answered by the passage?</u> |

Sample questions:

—What equipment has led to the new approach?

—What is an example of the approach taken in comparative planetology?

<u>Your definition</u> may look something like this (remember: this is just an example):

30

Filtration is a physical process used to separate mixtures into individual substances. It consists of pouring a mixture in which one of the substances is already liquid or has been dissolved to become liquid through a filter; this results in the liquid draining through the filter and the solid substance being caught by the filter.

The important point is this: does your answer contain the following information? That is, does it answer these questions?

What is the <u>topic</u>?

filtration

What is the <u>class</u>?

a physical process (for separating mixtures)

What is the <u>description</u>?

It consists of pouring a mixture. (See sample answer.)

Page Number	**Exercise Number**	**Answers (and Comments)**
		What is <u>relevance</u>?
		It is used to separate and purify mixtures.
30		"What is distillation?"
		Somewhere in your answer or definition the following information should appear.
		What is the <u>topic</u>?
		distillation
		What is the <u>class</u>?
		a physical process
		What is the <u>description</u>?
		It consists of boiling liquid mixtures, then collecting and condensing the vapors of the individual substances, which vaporize at different temperatures. Repeating the process increases the purity of the individual substances.
		What is the <u>relevance</u>?
		It is used to separate and purify mixtures.
32		Your definition of psychoanalysis should include the following information, however or wherever it may be expressed:
		What is the <u>topic</u>
		psychoanalysis

Page Number	**Exercise Number**	**Answers (and Comments)**

What is the <u>class</u>?

a method of psychotherapy

What is the <u>description</u>?

The method seeks to bring unconscious material to consciousness in clients through the use of such techniques as: free association, dream analysis, and transference.

What is the <u>relevance</u>?

It is used to try to help clients achieve insight into why they do what they do and think what they think..

32

Your definition of *catharsis* should include the following information, no matter how you choose to express it:

What is the <u>topic</u>?

catharsis

What is the <u>class</u>?

process

What is the <u>description</u>?

the release of pent-up emotions while unconscious thought processes are brought to consciousness

What is the <u>relevance</u>?

There is no other information beyond what is stated in the description.

Page Number	**Exercise Number**	**Answers (and Comments)**
32		Your definition of *free association* should include the following information, however or wherever it may be expressed:

What is the <u>topic</u>?

free association

What is the <u>class</u>?

a method used in psychoanalysis

What is the <u>description</u>?

The client lies on the couch, starts thinking about a particular symptom or problem, and then reports everything that comes to mind—a word, phrase, visual image. The client is not to omit anything, censor anything, or to worry about expressing thoughts in complete sentences. The therapist then processes and analyzes this information.

What is the <u>relevance</u>?

The last two lines of the excerpt begin to tell us, the readers, what the use of this method is. We can easily infer that the therapist will use the information in order to analyze the clients' problem.

33   Sample answer:

"Fascism is an ideology that asserts the supremacy of the nation or race over the interest of individuals or groups. It perceives the state as not merely a governmental bureaucracy but the organic life of a whole people."

Page Number	**Exercise Number**	**Answers (and Comments)**

The excerpt does not make any specific reference to relevance. The other three questions are answered.

34–39

No answer keys are provided for the five exercises on these pages since in some instances there is no one correct answer in terms of which exact words should be marked by an underline or a wavy line. The main purpose of the exercises is that you become even more aware about the different types of information you are finding—or not finding—as you read. After you have marked each passage we suggest that you

• review your own marking to see if, for example, the underlined words really do describe the topic rather than tell about its relevance or impact. Do they answer the question: "What is x?" and not "What is x useful for?" and not "What impact does x have?"

• compare with a classmate how each of you marked the passages. Even if you have different opinions about some parts of a passage, you will refine your understanding of description and relevance as you discuss them.

40

Topic: automatic stabilizers

Class: Government programs (thus stabilizers are a type of program)

Page Number	Exercise Number	Answers (and Comments)

41

Description: This information is provided by two examples of how two automatic stabilizers work; these two are income taxes and welfare programs. There is no general description of the characteristics.

Relevance: They are designed to counter the effects of economic cycles (and thus provide economic stability).

42

No answer key is provided for this exercise since in some instances there is no one correct answer in terms of which exact words should be marked by an underline or a wavy line. The main purpose of the exercises is that you become even more aware about the different types of information you are finding—or not finding—as you read. After you have marked each passage we suggest that you

- review your own marking to see if, for example, the underlined words really do describe the topic rather than tell about its relevance or impact. Do they answer the question: "What is x?" and not "What is x useful for?" and not "What impact does x have?"

- compare with a classmate how each of you marked the passages. Even if you have different opinions about some parts of a passage, you will refine your understanding of description and relevance as you discuss them.

Page Numbers	**Credits**
23, 39, 40	Thomas R. Dye, *Power and Society*, 5th ed., © 1990 by Harcourt Brace and Company. Reprinted by permission of the publisher.
25, 26, 27	William K. Hartman and Chris Impey, *Astronomy: The Cosmic Journey*, 5th ed., © 1994 by Wadsworth, Inc. Used by permission of the publisher.
29	G. Tyler Miller, Jr., *Chemistry: A Basic Introduction*, 4th ed., © 1987 Wadsworth, Inc.
30, 31, 34, 36, 37, 62–68	James W. Kalat, *Introduction to Psychology*. Copyright 1996, 1993, 1990, 1986 Wadsworth Publishing Company. Used by permission of Brooks/Cole Publishing Company, Pacific Grove, CA, a division of International Thomson Publishing Inc.
42	Andrew Cohen, *Language Learning*, 1990, Heinle and Heinle Publishers.

www.thecmcf.org

100, 25, 8-